Chinese Desserts Cookbook

30 Amazingly Delicious Traditional Chinese Dessert Recipes

BY

Carla Hale

Copyright 2019 Carla Hale

License Notes

No part of this Book can be reproduced in any form or by any means including print, electronic, scanning or photocopying unless prior permission is granted by the author.

All ideas, suggestions and guidelines mentioned here are written for informative purposes. While the author has taken every possible step to ensure accuracy, all readers are advised to follow information at their own risk. The author cannot be held responsible for personal and/or commercial damages in case of misinterpreting and misunderstanding any part of this Book

Table of Contents

Introduction 6

    Sweet Potato Soup 8

    Steamed Sponge Cake 10

    Milk Pudding 13

    Chines Pear and Date Soup 15

    Egg Tarts 17

    Pineapple Tarts 20

    Almond Cookies 23

    Butter Cookies 25

    Cashew Nut Egg Cookies 27

    Kuih Bahulu 30

    Shrimp Floss Pastry Rolls 32

    Red Bean Soup 34

    Fruity Wonton Stake 36

Mango Pudding 39

Tapioca Soup 41

Ginataang Bilo 43

Pumpkin Muffins 45

Almond Cake 47

Peanut Butter and Oats Balls 49

Pecan and Date Bars 51

Water Chestnut Chinese Pudding 53

Lilly Root Pudding 55

Peanut Candy 57

Mung Bean and Sago Soup 59

Sesame Seed Bars 61

Almond Pudding 63

Snow Balls 65

Melon Salad 67

Steamed Honey Pear 69

Coconut Milk and Bananas 71

Conclusion 73

Author's Afterthoughts.. 74

About the Author 75

Introduction

Chinese desserts are not only famous in China for their unique taste but are also famous all around the world. Now making delight full and soul satisfying Chinese dessert is not a tricky taste anymore. If you love eating Chinese deserts but afraid of trying these desserts then do not fell worry, because this book is going to be your best friend from today.

In this book all traditional and contemporary Chinese desserts are prepared for you which are going to be your favourite forever. In this book you are going to learn highly tasteful and tempting Chinese desserts which will make you pride in front of you loved ones. I hope you are going to love each and every recipe of this book.

So now let's get it started!

Sweet Potato Soup

This soup is super easy to make and yummy to taste.

Servings: 2

Cooking Time: 25 min

Ingredients

- 4 sweet potatoes, peeled, cubed
- 6 tablespoons brown sugar
- 4 cups water
- 1-inch ginger slice

Directions

1. In a saucepan add water, sugar, ginger, sweet potatoes, mix well. Cover and cook on medium heat for 20-25 minutes.

2. Make sure that sweet potatoes are softened.

3. Enjoy.

Steamed Sponge Cake

This cake is super soft and extraordinary delicious.

Servings: 5

Cooking Time: 25 min

Ingredients

- 6 eggs
- 1 1⁄2 cup all-purpose flour
- 1 cup caster sugar
- 1 teaspoon baking powder
- 1 pinch slat
- 1 teaspoon vanilla extract

Directions

1. In a large saucepan add 3 cups of water and let to boil. Place a trivet in saucepan.

2. Meanwhile beat eggs until fully.

3. Now add in sugar and beat again for 1-2 minutes.

4. Now add in flour, salt, vanilla extract, and baking powder, mix with spatula.

5. Pour mixture in a parchment lined deep baking pan.

6. Place it on trivet and cover with lid.

7. Let to cook for 20-25 minutes.

8. Serve when cooled.

Milk Pudding

Make this mouth-melting pudding today and enjoy with your whole family.

Servings: 4

Cooking Time: 15 min

Ingredients

- 8 egg whites
- 1 litter milk
- 1 cup sugar

Directions

1. In a mixing bowl add milk and sugar, beat with electric beat until foam appears at the surface.

2. Take another bowl and beat egg white until fluff.

3. Now combine egg white with milk mixture.

4. Take a deep pan and add in mixture. Cover pan with food wrapper.

5. Place it in steamer and let to cook for 15 minutes.

6. Enjoy.

Chines Pear and Date Soup

This soup is sweetened with dates without sugar.

Servings: 2

Cooking Time: 120 min

Ingredients

- 2 chines pear, peeled, cubes
- 8-10 dates, stoned
- 1 cup dried longans, drained
- 4 cups of water

Directions

1. In a slow cooked add water, pears, and dates, cover and cook on high for 1 hour.

2. Now open the lid and add in longans, cook again for another 1 hour.

3. Serve hot.

4. Enjoy.

Egg Tarts

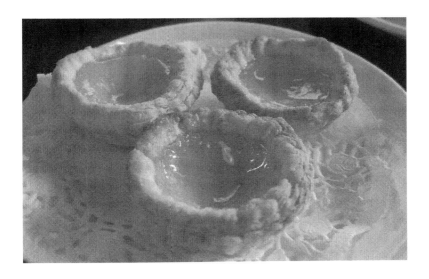

These egg tarts are going to be your favourite ones.

Servings: 12

Cooking Time: 25 min

Ingredients

- ¼ cup hot water
- 2 cups all-purpose flour
- 4 eggs
- 1 ¼ cup vegetable shortening
- 2 cups milk
- 1 teaspoon slat
- ¾ cup sugar

Directions

1. Preheat oven at 180 degrees C.

2. In a bowl add flour, salt, and vegetable shortening, mix until crumbs are made.

3. Add in water and knead a soft dough.

4. Roll out dough on a floured surface into 18-inch thick sheet.

5. Cut into 12-14 circles.

6. Place the circles in greased muffin cups.

7. In a bowl combine sugar, eggs, and milk, mix well.

8. Pour mixture in pastry muffins.

9. Bake for 25 minutes.

10. Enjoy when done.

Pineapple Tarts

Your kids will love these tarts for sure.

Servings: 12

Cooking Time: 20 min

Ingredients

- 1 cup pineapple jam
- ¾ cup caster sugar
- ½ cup butter, cold
- 1 egg, beaten
- 1 cup all-purpose flour
- 2-3 drops of vanilla essence

Directions

1. In a bowl add flour and butter, mix with hands until crumbled.

2. Take a bowl and add in sugar, vanilla, and eggs, mix until combined.

3. Combine with flour mixture. Knead a dough and cover with plastic wrap. Place in refrigerator for 20 minutes.

4. Now roll out dough on a floured surface in 0.5cm thick sheet.

5. Cut with tart mold.

6. Top them with 1 teaspoon of jam. Place them at the lower most shelf of oven.

7. Let to bake for 20 minutes.

Almond Cookies

These delightful cookies are made up with roasted almonds.

Servings: 10

Cooking Time: 40 min

Ingredients

- 1 cup all-purpose flour
- 2 teaspoons baking powder
- 1 ½ teaspoon salt
- 2 cups roasted almonds, powdered
- ¼ cup cooking oil
- 1 cup caster sugar
- Egg wash combined with some salt

Directions

1. In a large mixing bowl add flour, sugar, salt, cooking oil, almonds, and baking powder, mix well and knead a smooth dough.

2. Make small balls with the dough and place them in greased baking tray.

3. Brush with egg wash.

4. Bake for 40 minutes or until nicely cooked.

5. Enjoy.

Butter Cookies

You are going to fall in love with these cookies.

Servings: 12

Cooking Time: 45 min

Ingredients

- 1 cup cake flour
- ¼ cup icing sugar
- ¼ cup white sugar
- 1 egg
- 1-2 drops of vanilla essence
- ½ cup butter, melted

Directions

1. In a mixing bowl add icing sugar and butter, beat until creamy. Add in egg and beat again for 1-2 minutes.

2. Now add flour, white sugar, and vanilla essence, mix well.

3. Put mixture in piping bag.

4. Pipe out in greased baking tray and bake for 45 minutes.

5. Enjoy.

Cashew Nut Egg Cookies

These cookies are made with crumbled cashew nuts, egg yolks, and butter.

Servings: 10

Cooking Time: 25 min

Ingredients

- 2 cups cake flour
- 1 cup cashew nuts, roasted
- ½ cup butter, melted
- ¾ cup icing sugar
- ¼ cup milk powder
- 3 egg yolks
- Egg wash and some cashew nuts for topping

Directions

1. Preheat oven at 150-degrees C.

2. In a food processor add cashew nuts and process until crumbled.

3. Transfer in a bowl and combine with flour, milk powder, butter, icing sugar, and egg yolk, knead a smooth dough.

4. Roll put on a floured surface in 1/8-inch-thick sheet and cut with cookie cutter.

5. Transfer cooking in greased baking tray and brush them with egg wash, place cashes on top.

6. Bake for 25 minutes.

7. Enjoy when done.

Kuih Bahulu

This traditional Chinese delight can be made in few minutes.

Servings: 4

Cooking Time: 10 min

Ingredients

- 4 eggs
- 1 teaspoon vanilla essence
- 1 cup icing sugar
- 1 cup all-purpose flour

Directions

1. In a mixing bowl add icing sugar, eggs, and vanilla essence beat until creamy and fluffy.

2. Greases the kuih bahulu mold with cooking oil and place them in oven at 200 degrees C.

3. Now add flour in egg mixture and mix well.

4. Fill mold with batter and let to cook in oven for 10 minutes.

5. Enjoy when done.

Shrimp Floss Pastry Rolls

These pastry rolls are filled up with yummy shrimp's floss.

Servings: 20-25

Cooking Time: 15 min

Ingredients

- 8 pastry sheets
- 1 cup shrimp floss
- 3 tablespoons of corn flour combined with 4 tablespoons of water

Directions

1. Cut each puff pastry sheet into 4 equal spares.

2. Place some shrimp floss at the centre of each square and brush the edges with corn flour mixture. Roll up. Make sure that edges are locked well.

3. Now place them in baking tray and bake for 15 minutes.

4. Serve and enjoy.

Red Bean Soup

This dessert is easy to make and tasty to eat.

Servings: 4

Cooking Time: 90 min

Ingredients

- 1 ½ cup red beans, soaked in water, overnight
- 8 cups of water
- 1 strip of orange peel
- ½ cup brown sugar
- ¼ cup lotus seeds, soaked in water for 2 hours

Directions

1. In a saucepan add water and orange peel, let to boil well.

2. Add in beans and lotus seeds, reduce flame and cook covered for 2 hours.

3. Add in sugar and mix well, cook again for another 30 minutes.

4. Discard orange peel when serving.

5. Enjoy.

Fruity Wonton Stake

These Wontons are not only easy to make but yummy.

Servings: 8

Cooking Time: 5 min

Ingredients

- 16 wonton wraps
- 1 cup milk
- ¼ cup coconut milk
- ¾ cup sugar
- ¼ cup custard powder mixed with 3 tablespoons of water
- 1 cup strawberries, sliced
- 1 cup passion fruit, sliced
- 1 teaspoon olive oil

Directions

1. Preheat oven at 150 degrees C.

2. Place wontons in greased baking tray and drizzle some olive oil on them, bake for 5 minutes or until crisp.

3. In a saucepan boil milk and add in sugar.

4. Add I coconut milk and custard mixture, stir until thickened.

5. Set aside until cooled.

6. Now spread a wonton in each serving platter and top it with custard, fruits and finely another wonton.

7. Enjoy.

Mango Pudding

This pudding is made up with mango puree and evaporated milk.

Servings: 4

Cooking Time: 0 min

Ingredients

- 4 large mangoes, peeled, sliced
- ¼ cup hot water
- ½ cup sugar
- 10 ice cubes
- 2 ½ tablespoons Gelatin
- 1 ½ cup evaporated milk

Directions

1. In a blender mango and blend well until puree.

2. In a bowl combine sugar, water, and Gelatin. Stir until sugar is dissolved.

3. Now combine mango puree with sugar mixture and ad in ice cubes.

4. Add in milk and mix well.

5. Transfer mixture in ramekins and place in freezer for 4-5 hours.

6. Enjoy.

Tapioca Soup

Make this delightful soup today and surprise everyone.

Servings: 4

Cooking Time: 30 min

Ingredients

- 1 ½ cup tapioca pearls
- 1 cup sugar
- 5+2 cups water
- 8 ounces of yam, peeled, diced
- 1 can of coconut milk

Directions

1. In a saucepan add 5 cups of water and let to boil.

2. Add in tapioca and stir until transparent or about 10-15 minutes on medium heat.

3. Now drain and rinse with cold water, set aside.

4. In a saucepan add 2 cups of water, sugar, and yam, cook until boiled.

5. Now add in coconut milk and tapioca. Mix well. Turn off heat.

6. Serve hot.

7. Enjoy.

Ginataang Bilo

This dish is made glutinous balls and sago pearls.

Servings: 8

Cooking Time: 45 min

Ingredients

- 1 cup sago pearls
- 6 cups coconut mil
- 1 ½ cup coconut cream
- 2 cups jackfruit, sliced
- 1 cup white sugar
- 18-19 glutinous rice balls

Directions

1. In a saucepan add 8 cups of water and let to boil.

2. Add in sago pearls and cook until transparent. Drain and rinse with cold water, set aside.

3. In a saucepan add milk and sugar, mix until sugar is dissolved.

4. Add in rice balls and coo for 6-7 minutes.

5. Now add in cream, jackfruit, and sago pearls, mix well. Let to simmer for 3-4 minutes.

6. Serve hot and enjoy.

Pumpkin Muffins

These uniquely flavoured pumpkin muffins are steamed.

Servings: 8

Cooking Time: 15 min

Ingredients

- 2 eggs
- 1 cup milk
- 1 cup pumpkin puree
- ½ cup rice flour
- 1 teaspoon baking powder
- ¼ teaspoon baking soda
- 1 cup all-purpose flour
- ¾ cup caster sugar

Directions

1. In a mixing bowl add all ingredients and whisk well.

2. In a saucepan add 2 cups of water and let to boil. Place a tritave in saucepan.

3. Fill greased muffin cups with batter and place on tritave.

4. Cover saucepan with lid and leave to cook for 15 minutes.

5. Enjoy.

Almond Cake

Make this delight today and blow everyone's mind.

Servings: 4

Cooking Time: 35 min

Ingredients

- 4 eggs
- 2 cups almond flour
- 1 cup sugar
- 1 teaspoon baking powder
- 1 cup lard

Directions

1. Take a bowl and add in almond flour, sugar, baking powder, and eggs, mix well.

2. Gradually add lard and mix well.

3. Preheat oven at 355 degrees.

4. Transfer batter in greased baking pan and bake for 30-35 minutes.

5. Enjoy.

Peanut Butter and Oats Balls

This dessert can be made in glance.

Servings: 6

Cooking Time: 0 min

Ingredients

- 1 cup oats
- 4 tablespoons honey
- 2 tablespoons peanut butter
- 2 tablespoons coconut oil, melted
- ¼ teaspoon cinnamon powder
- 2 tablespoons hot water
- ¼ cup dates, stoned

Directions

1. In a blender add all ingredients and blend until combined.

2. Now make round balls with mixture and place them in platter.

3. Transfer in refrigerator for 3-4 hours.

4. Enjoy.

Pecan and Date Bars

Make these yummy date and pecan bars and share with your loved ones.

Servings: 6

Cooking Time: 10 min

Ingredients

- 2 cups milk
- 2 cups dates, chopped
- 1 cup pecans, chopped
- 2-3 drops of vanilla
- ¼ cup butter
- ½ brown cup sugar

Directions

1. In a saucepan add milk, sugar, butter, dates, and pecan, let it to boil.

2. Cook until everything is combined and milk is thickened.

3. Now remove from heat and stir in vanilla.

4. Spread batter on parchment lined baking tray.

5. Let to cool in refrigerator for 1-2 hours.

6. Now cut in desired shape.

Water Chestnut Chinese Pudding

This dessert is the great combination water chestnuts powder, water, and sugar.

Servings: 3

Cooking Time: 60 min

Ingredients

- 3 cups water chestnuts powder
- 1 ½ cup sugar
- 7 cups of water

Directions

1. In a bowl add water and sugar, mix until dissolved.

2. Now add in water chestnuts powder and stir well.

3. Pour mixture in a deep pan.

4. Place this mixture in streamer and cook for 60 minutes, covered.

5. Enjoy when done.

Lilly Root Pudding

This delight is made up with lily root powder and water.

Servings: 6

Cooking Time: 60 min

Ingredients

- 2 ½ cups lily root powder
- 1 ½ cup sugar
- 8 cups of water

Directions

1. In a mixing bowl add water and lily root powder, let to dissolve for few minutes.

2. Now add sugar and whisk until sugar is mixed.

3. Pour mixture in a pan and place it in steamer.

4. Let to cook for 55-60 minutes.

5. Enjoy.

Peanut Candy

Enjoy making this uniquely flavoured candy and surprise your kids.

Servings: 8

Cooking Time: 20 min

Ingredients

- 2 cups sugar
- 1 cup water
- 1 cup peanuts, roasted
- 3 tablespoons butter

Directions

1. In a saucepan add water and sugar, stir until combined.

2. Let to cook until colour of sugar is changed to lightly golden.

3. Now add peanuts and butter mix quickly.

4. Transfer mixture in greased baking tray.

5. Let to cool.

6. Now cut in desired shape.

7. Enjoy.

Mung Bean and Sago Soup

This soup will satisfy your soul.

Servings: 4

Cooking Time: 35 min

Ingredients

- 1 can coconut milk
- 1 cup sago pearls, soaked in water for 15 minutes
- 1 ¼ cup mung beans
- 7 cups of water
- 1 cup brown sugar

Directions

1. In a saucepan add water, mung beans, and, let to cook covered on low heat for 30 minutes.

2. Add in brown sugar and sago pearls, stir until sugar is dissolved.

3. Simmer for 10 minutes.

4. Serve and enjoy.

Sesame Seed Bars

These bars are made up with sugar and sesame seeds.

Servings: 6

Cooking Time: 15 min

Ingredients

- 2 cups sugar
- 1 cup water
- 1 cup white sesame seeds
- ½ cup black sesame seeds

Directions

1. In a pan add sugar and water, stir until boiled.

2. Now when the colour of sugar is changed and it becomes sticky add in sesame seeds, mix quickly.

3. Transfer mixture in greased baking tray and spread well.

4. Let to cool.

5. Cut into desired shape.

6. Enjoy.

Almond Pudding

This pudding is delightful which is easy to make.

Servings: 2

Cooking Time: 15 min

Ingredients

- 2 cups coconuts, soaked in water overnight
- ¼ cup rice, soaked in water for 1 hour
- 5 tablespoons sugar
- 1 egg white
- 2 cups water

Directions

1. Peel the soaked almonds and transfer them in food processor with water, rice and sugar. Blend until puree.

2. Now transfer mixture in a saucepan and let to cook for 15 minutes. Stir continuously.

3. Add in egg white and stir well. Remove from heat.

4. Place in refrigerator for 1-2 hours before serving.

5. Enjoy.

Snow Balls

These balls are made up with sweet potato puree and glutinous rice, coated with coconut.

Servings: 8

Cooking Time: 2 min

Ingredients

- 3 large sweet potatoes, peeled, puree
- 1 cup caster sugar
- 2 cups glutinous rice flour
- 1 cup coconut, shredded

Directions

1. In a bowl add sweet potato puree, sugar, and rice flour, mix well until a smooth dough is made.

2. Make round balls with dough and place them in a platter.

3. In a sauce an add 3-4 cups of water and let to boil.

4. Drop balls in boiling water and cook them for 2 minutes.

5. Now remove from water and roll them in shredded coconut.

6. Enjoy.

Melon Salad

You have to try out this dessert if you want a quick and refreshing delight.

Servings: 3

Cooking Time: 0 min

Ingredients

- 2 cups honeydew melon balls
- 2 cups cantaloupe balls
- 2 cups watermelon balls
- 4 tablespoons icing sugar
- ¼ cup honey
- 3-4 mint leaves, chopped

Directions

1. In a bowl add honey, sugar and minx leaves mix well.

2. Add in all fruits and toss to combine.

3. Transfer to serving bowl.

4. Serve and enjoy.

Steamed Honey Pear

Make this dessert today and surprize everyone.

Servings: 2

Cooking Time: 30 min

Ingredients

- 2 pears, peeled
- 4 tablespoons honey

Directions

1. Drizzle honey on both pears until coated well.

2. Place them in steamer basket and steam for 30 minutes covered.

3. Enjoy when done.

Coconut Milk and Bananas

Your kids are going to fall in love with this yummy dessert.

Servings: 2

Cooking Time: 10 min

Ingredients

- 4 cups coconut milk
- 1 pinch cinnamon powder
- ½ cup sugar
- 2 bananas, peeled, sliced

Directions

1. In a saucepan add milk and sugar, let to boil well.

2. Add In bananas and cinnamon powder, mxi well, simmer for 5 minutes.

3. Serve and enjoy.

Conclusion

Wow we did it! Thank you for sticking through all the way the end of the Chinese Dessert Cookbook with us. We hope you enjoyed all 30 mouth-watering Chinese dessert recipes that are perfect for any meal.

So, what happens next?

Nothing breathes perfection like practice. So, keep on cooking and enjoying new and exciting meals with your whole family. Then whenever you are ready for another spark of delicious inspiration grab another one of our books and let us continue our culinary journey together.

Remember, drop us a review if you loved what you read and until we meet again, keep on cooking delicious food.

Author's Afterthoughts

Thanks Ever So Much to Each of My Cherished Readers for Investing the Time to Read This Book!

I know you could have picked from many other books but you chose this one. So, big thanks for buying this book and reading all the way to the end.

If you enjoyed this book or received value from it, I'd like to ask you for a favor. Please take a few minutes to post an honest and heartfelt review on Amazon. Your support does make a difference and helps to benefit other people.

Thank you!

Carla Hale

About the Author

Carla Hale

I think of myself as a foodie. I like to eat, yes. I like to cook even more. I like to prepare meals for my family and friends, I feel like that's what I was born to do...

My name is Carla Hale and as may have suspected already, I am originally from Scotland. I am first and foremost a mother, a wife, but simultaneously over the years I became a proclaimed cook. I have shared my recipes with many and will continue to do so, as long as I can. I like different. I dress different, I love different, I speak different and I cook different. I like to think that I am different because I am more animated about what I do than most; I feel more and care more.

It served me right when cooking to sprinkle some tenderness, love, passion, in every dish I prepare. It does not matter if I am preparing a meal for strangers passing by my cooking booth at the flea market or if I am making my mother's favorite recipe. Each and every meal I prepare from scratch will contain a little bite of my life story and little part of my heart in it. People feel it, taste it and ask for more! Thank you for taking the time to get to know me and hopefully through my recipes you can learn a lot more about my influences and preferences. Who knows you might just find your own favorite within my repertoire! Enjoy!